GOAL!

THE HOCKEY COLORING BOOK

Arkady Roytman

DOVER PUBLICATIONS, INC.
Mineola, New York

Note

The sport of hockey is one of the most popular games in the world and in this exciting and informative coloring book artist Arkady Roytman has created 30 illustrations capturing the history, action, and excitement of this ancient sport. From hockey's origins as shinty to the famous "Miracle on Ice" in the 1980 Olympic Games, this book showcases all of the great moments and great players in the annals of hockey.

Copyright

Copyright © 2013 by Dover Publications, Inc.
All rights reserved.

Bibliographical Note

GOAL! The Hockey Coloring Book is a new work, first published by
Dover Publications, Inc., in 2013.

International Standard Book Number

ISBN-13: 978-0-486-49889-8
ISBN-10: 0-486-49889-1

Manufactured in the United States by LSC Communications
49889106   2017
www.doverpublications.com

Shinty – A Scottish form of "field hockey" played with a ball and a wooden stick called a "caman," shinty was first played on ice in 1800 by Scottish immigrants in Nova Scotia, Canada.

Bandy –With rules similar to those of association football (soccer), bandy is played on the ice with each team having 11 players, including a goalkeeper. There were two versions of the game originally, one from England and the other from Russia.

Lacrosse – A Native American game originating about 1100 AD, lacrosse means "the stick" in French. In the Native American version, it used to be played with as many as 1000 participants and go on for two or three days.

Rugby – Although not a stick and ball game, rugby's rules, especially not allowing the throwing of the ball forward, were the model for the first organized hockey game.

First Organized Indoor Game - On March 3, 1875, James Creighton and several McGill University students organized the first indoor game of hockey at Montreal's Victoria Skating Rink. A puck was used instead of a ball to prevent it from exiting the rink, which did not have boards.

1920 Winnipeg Falcons – Hockey was introduced to the Olympics in the summer games of 1920. Canada's Winnipeg Falcons won the first-ever hockey Olympic gold medal.

1956 USSR Team – In their Olympic hockey debut, the Soviet team won the gold medal. It went on to win four consecutive Olympic gold medals (1964, 1968, 1972, and 1976) and nine consecutive World Championships and was nicknamed "The Big Red Machine."

1972 Summit Series - Canada vs USSR - Probably the most well known moment in hockey history, Paul Henderson's goal with mere seconds remaining brought a nation to its feet as Canada took down the hockey superpower that was the Soviet team.

Miracle on Ice -1980 Olympics - Voted the greatest sports moment of the twentieth century by *Sports Illustrated*, a relatively inexperienced American hockey team squared off against the mighty Soviets and won.

Women's Hockey League – During World War I, when most of the male hockey players shipped off to fight in Europe, audiences flocked to watch women play. They were often times more ruthless than the male players.

The Great One

Wayne Gretzky

Wayne Gretzky (The Great One) – The Canadian hockey legend Wayne Gretzky started his professional career in 1978 and at the time of his retirement in 1999 held 40 regular-season records, 6 All-Star records and 15 playoff records. He is the only NHL player to total over 200 points in one season, which he accomplished 4 times.

Bobby Orr

Bobby Orr – One of the NHL's best defenseman, Bobby Orr scored what may be the most famous goal of all time in sudden death overtime against the St. Louis Blues in Game 4 of the 1970 Stanley Cup Finals. His injury-shortened career lasted 12 years, starting in 1966.

Gordie Howe
Mr. Hockey

Gordie Howe (Mr. Hockey) - Beginning his player career in 1946, Gordie Howe happens to be the only player to have competed in the NHL in 5 different decades (1940s through 1980s). He held the record for the most points in a career until he was surpassed by Wayne Gretzky and Mark Messier.

Hockey Rink - A standard rink in North America is 200 feet long and 85 feet wide, with goal lines 11 feet from the end boards.

In most European venues, the ice is 197 feet long and 98 feet wide and the goal lines are 13 feet from the end boards. International games also use only one on-ice referee instead of two.

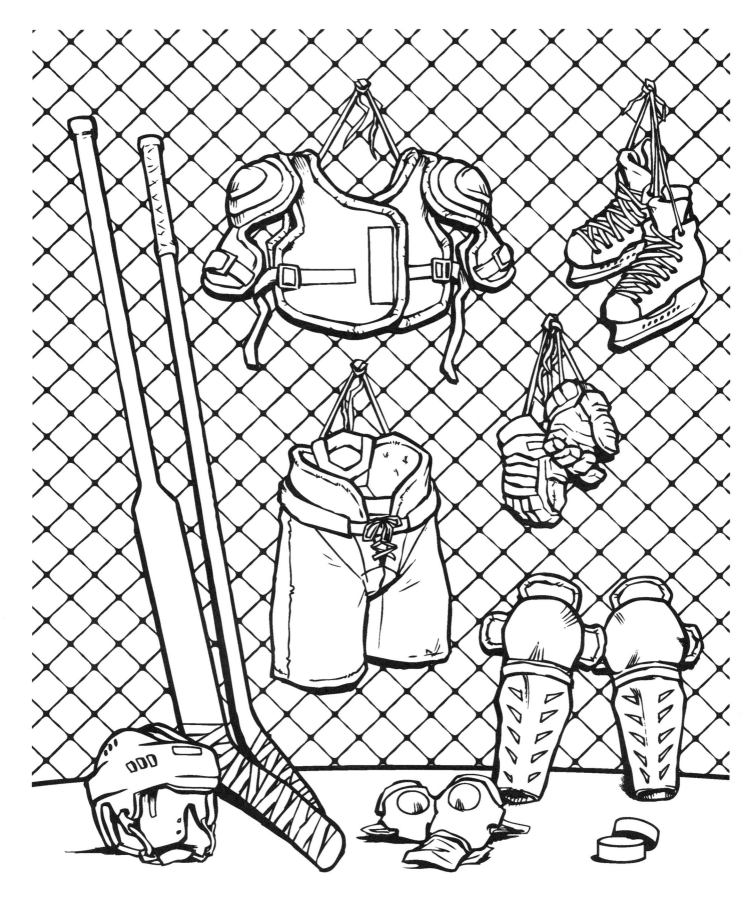

Equipment – Because the game is so rough, protective equipment is worn and includes a helmet, shoulder pads, elbow pads, mouth guard, protective gloves, heavily padded shorts (also known as hockey pants), athletic cup, shin pads, skates, and (optionally) a neck protector.

Goalie - Goaltenders use different gear, a neck guard, chest/arm protector, blocker, catch glove, and leg pads. Under NHL rules, goaltenders cannot handle the puck behind the goal line, except in the area directly behind the net. Goaltenders in international hockey can play the puck anywhere behind the net.

The Players - Five players other than the goaltender are typically divided into three forwards and two defensemen. Forwards often play together as units or lines, with the same three forwards always playing together.

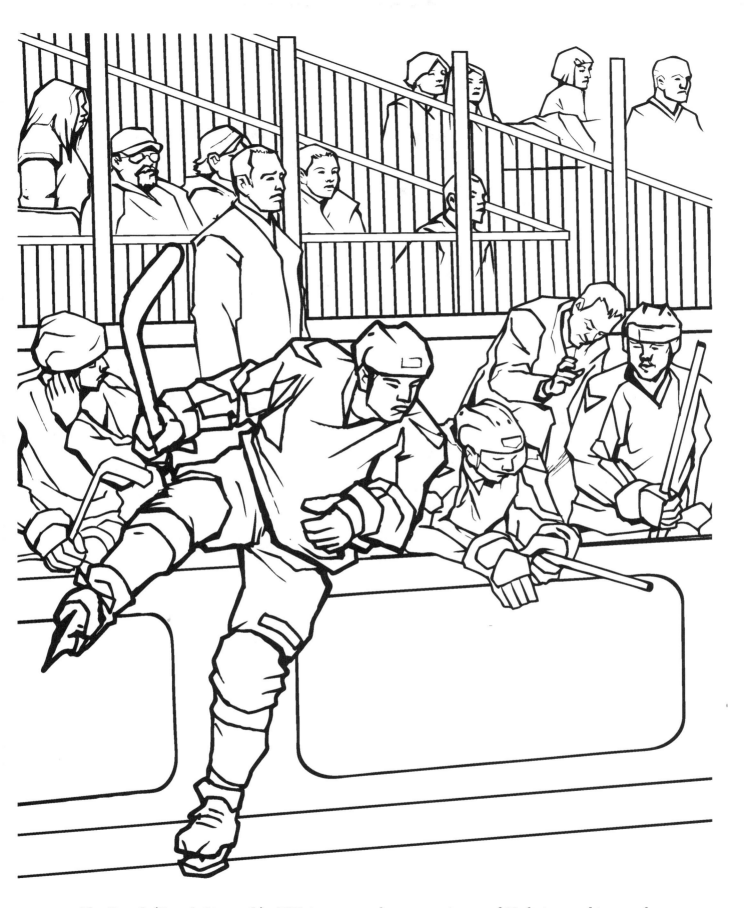

The Bench (Bench Strength) - NHL teams can dress a maximum of 18 skaters and two goal-tenders for a game. International rules allow a maximum of 20 skaters and two goaltenders on each team.

Faceoff - When play is stopped, it is restarted with a faceoff. Two players "face" each other and an official drops the puck to the ice, where the two players attempt to gain control of it.

Body Check - Players are permitted to "body check" opponents into the boards as a means of stopping progress.

GOAL!!! - A goal is scored when the puck completely crosses the goal line between the two goal posts and below the goal crossbar. A goal awards one point to the team attacking the net scored upon, regardless of which team the player who actually deflected the puck into the goal belongs to.

Penalty Box – A power play is when at least one opposing player is serving a penalty, and the team has a numerical advantage on the ice (whenever both teams have the same number of penalties being served, there is no power play). Up to two players per side may serve in the penalty box, giving a team up to a possible 5-on-3 power play. If a goaltender commits a foul, another player who was on the ice at the time of the penalty serves. A power play resulting from a simple minor penalty ends if the attacking team scores.

Icing –This infraction occurs when a player shoots the puck across at least two red lines and the puck remains untouched. When icing occurs, a linesman stops play. Play is resumed with a faceoff in the defending zone of the team that committed the infraction. In the NHL, an opposing player must touch the puck first before icing is called. International hockey uses "no touch" icing. The play is whistled down as soon as the puck crosses the goal line.

Fighting - NHL gives only a 5 minute penalty for fighting, whereas the Olympic rules call for a match penalty and possible ejection from the game. Fighting during an International game leads to the involved players sitting out the rest of the game, not just penalty time.

The Shootout - In the Olympics, tied playoff games are followed by ten minutes of sudden death overtime. If the game remains tied, it is decided by a shootout. The NHL has adopted the shootout for regular season games only. During the Stanley Cup Playoffs, teams play overtime until a tie-breaking goal is scored.

Slapshot - The hardest shot in ice hockey, a slapshot starts with a wind up and continues with the player violently "slapping" the ice slightly behind the puck. The player uses his weight to bend the stick, storing energy in it like a spring. This bending of the stick gives the slapshot its amazing speed

Women In Hockey - Ice hockey is one of the fastest growing women's sports in the world, with the number of participants increasing 350 percent in the last 10 years. The main difference between women's and men's ice hockey is that body checking is not allowed in women's ice hockey.

Stanley Cup - In 1892, realizing that there was no recognition for the best team in all of Canada, the Governor General of Canada, Lord Stanley of Preston, purchased a decorative bowl for use as a trophy. The Dominion Hockey Challenge Cup, which later became more famously known as the Stanley Cup, was first awarded in 1893 to the Montreal Hockey Club.

Hockey Hall of Fame - 1961: The Hockey Hall of Fame opens in Toronto.